PROFESSOR ASTRO CAT'S
STARGAZING

DR DOMINIC WALLIMAN & BEN NEWMAN

•FLYING EYE BOOKS•

LONDON | NEW YORK

BRIGHT LIGHTS

If you look up into the night sky, you can see hundreds of tiny, shining lights scattered everywhere. These are called stars!

PROFESSOR
ASTRO CAT

THE SPEED OF LIGHT

Even though light is the fastest thing in the Universe, it still takes the light from stars an incredibly long time to reach Earth.

The distance that light can travel in one year is called a **light year**. If you had to walk one light year, it would take you about 225 million years! Even your grandparents aren't that old!

Most stars are so far away that the light you see from them today actually left those stars millions of years ago. That means that looking into space is like looking into the past!

WHAT IS A STAR?

A star is an enormous ball of burning gas in outer space, which gives out lots of energy. You can see and feel this energy through heat and light.

Don't get too close though – this star is incredibly hot. In fact, most stars are millions of times hotter than a kitchen oven!

The gas that makes up a star is held together by **gravity**. Gravity holds all objects in the Universe together. It's what pulls you back to Earth when you jump up into the air!

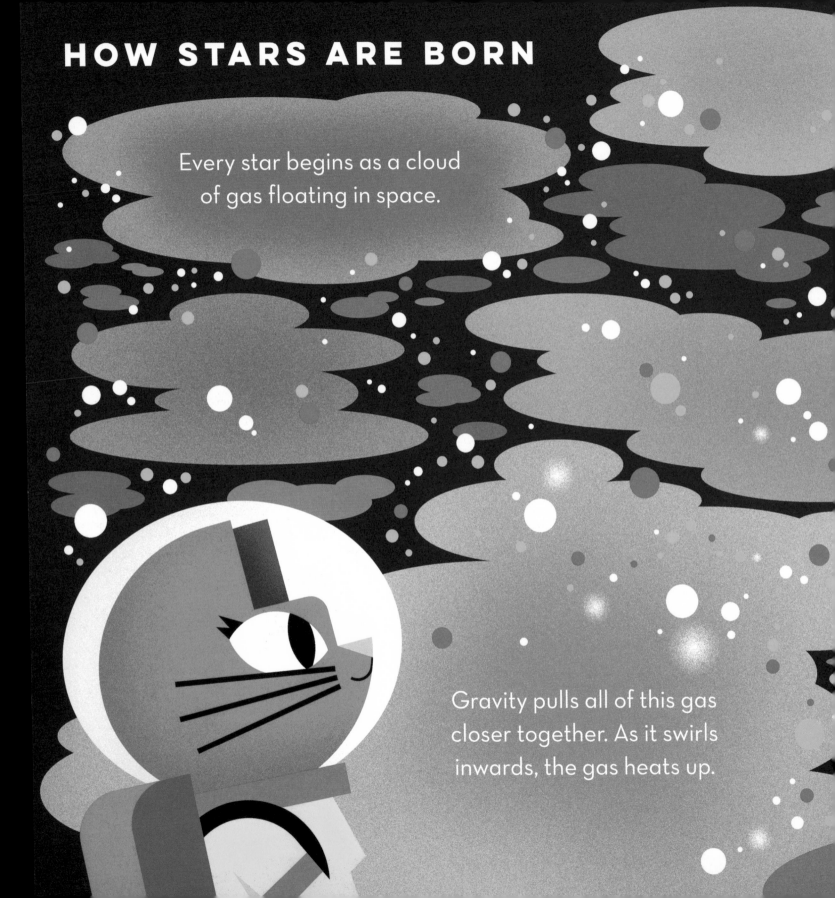

HOW STARS ARE BORN

Every star begins as a cloud
of gas floating in space.

Gravity pulls all of this gas
closer together. As it swirls
inwards, the gas heats up.

The gas gets closer and closer and hotter and hotter until ... boom! In a flash of light and heat, a star is born!

One star is so close that we can see it during the day. In fact, it gives us daylight! Yes, our incredible Sun is a star too.

TYPES OF STARS

Most stars in the Universe look very
similar, but not all stars are the same.
Our Sun is called a 'main sequence star'.

This is a 'giant star'. These stars are bigger, hotter and brighter than most other stars. They burn lots of energy quickly, so their lifespan is shorter than other stars.

Here, we have a 'red dwarf star'. These tiny stars are not that bright, so they burn energy slowly. This means they live for a very, very long time!

THE END OF A STAR

Even stars don't live for ever! As time goes by, they run out of energy and start to die.

WHITE DWARF

NEUTRON STAR

Eventually, the stars collapse – some into tiny bright stars called white dwarfs and others into neutron stars.

The biggest stars end their lives with a huge explosion called a **supernova.** Some supernovae are so strong that they tear a hole in space itself, making a **black hole**!

GALAXIES

Stars tend to stick together in groups called **galaxies**. The planets, the Sun and most of the stars you can see in the sky are part of our galaxy.

OUR SOLAR SYSTEM IN THE MILKY WAY

Our galaxy is called the **Milky Way**.
You can sometimes see a part of it from Earth
as a big, sparkling streak in the night sky.

Like stars, all galaxies are different.
Some are big, jumbled groups, while others,
like ours, look a bit like pinwheels.

DISTANT STARS

Here we have the Andromeda galaxy.
It is the nearest galaxy to ours, though it
is still millions of light years away.

**ANDROMEDA
GALAXY**

The light from this galaxy has been
travelling for such a long time that
what we see today is actually how
it looked before humans existed!

Andromeda is one of the few galaxies we can see from Earth, but there are millions of other galaxies even further away in deep, dark space.

TAKING A CLOSER LOOK

We can study distant stars with **telescopes**.
They let us see faraway items more closely.

Some telescopes are small enough to place next to your bedroom window, but some are so big that they require their own special building called an **observatory**.

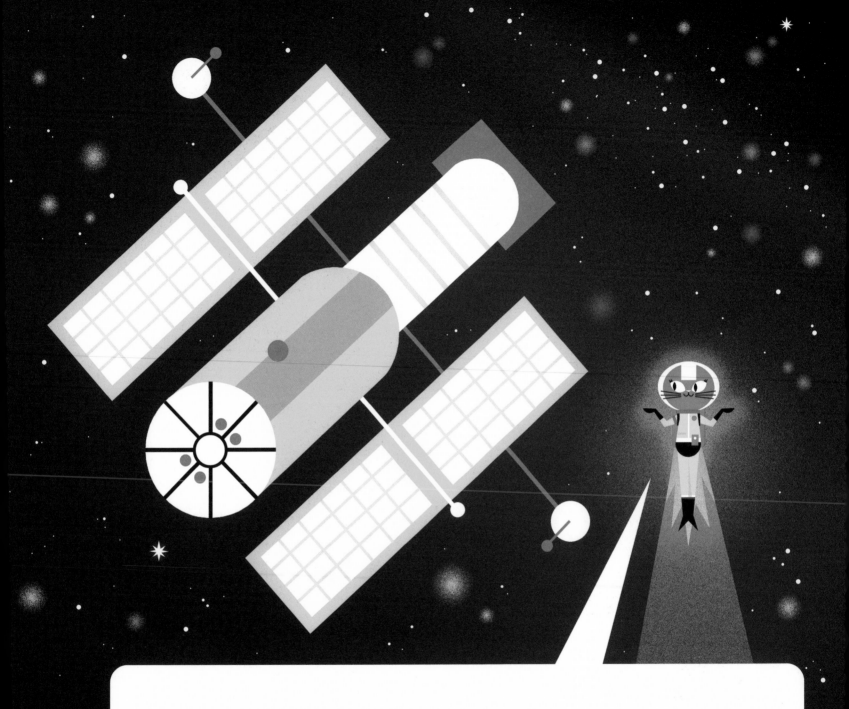

The **Hubble Space Telescope** is special because it is
floating in space right now. It takes beautiful photographs
of faraway galaxies and sends them back to us on Earth.

STARGAZING

You don't need a telescope to gaze at stars in the night sky. A long time ago, people would look up and play connect-the-dots with stars to make pictures.

CYGNUS

URSA MAJOR

CANIS MINOR

PEGASUS

These pictures are called **constellations**. They are named after characters from famous stories, like Pegasus the flying horse or Leo the lion!

CANCER

LYRA

LEO

ORION

Earth is always moving, so you will see different stars at different times of the year. If you can't find a constellation now, try again in a few months!

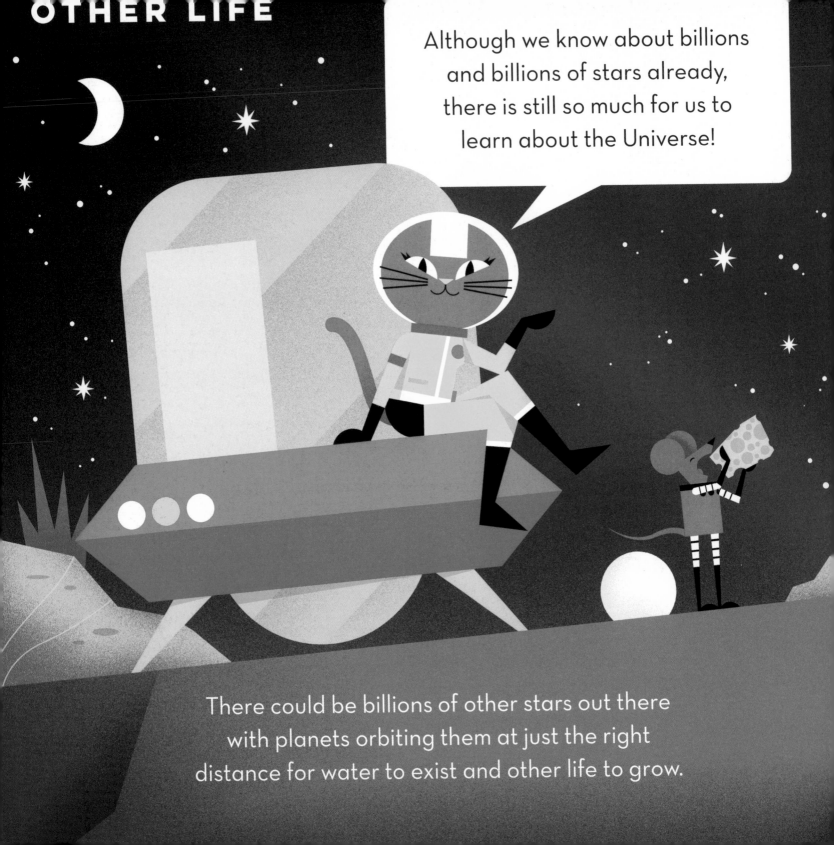

It's up to future space explorers like you to discover new information about the Universe. Until next time, my fellow stargazers, knowledge awaits!

GLOSSARY

Black hole A hole in space formed when big stars collapse. Gravity is so strong here that nothing, not even light, can escape.

Constellation A group of stars that are named after something they resemble.

Galaxy A group of millions of stars held together by gravity.

Gravity The force that keeps us planted on Earth and keeps items in space.

Hubble Space Telescope A famous telescope that takes photographs in space.